Secrets To Planning The Perfect Speech For Politicians

How To Plan To Give The Best Speech Of Your Life!

"Practical, proven techniques that will help you to make your next speech a success"

Dr. Jim Anderson

Published by

Blue Elephant Consulting

Tampa, Florida

Printed in the United States of America

Library of Congress Control Number: 2017906867

ISBN-13: 978-1546423638
ISBN-10: 154642363X

Warning – Disclaimer

Other Books By The Author

Product Management

- Manage Your Customers, Manage Your Product: Techniques For Product Managers To Better Understand What Their Customers Really Want

- Managing Your Product Manager Career: How Product Managers Can Find And Succeed In The Right Job

Public Speaking

- How To Get Ready To Give The Perfect Speech: What Tools To Use To Create Your Next Speech So That Your Message Will Be Remembered Forever!

- Creating Speeches That Work: How To Create A Speech That Will Make Your Message Be Remembered Forever!

CIO Skills

- How CIOs Can Take Their Career To The Next Level: How CIOs Can Work With The Entire Company In Order To Be Successful

- How CIOs Can Bring Business And IT Together: How CIOs Can Use Their Technical Skills To Help Their

Company Solve Real-World Business Problems

IT Manager Skills

- Understanding What Leadership Means For IT Managers: Tips And Techniques That IT Managers Can Use In Order To Develop Leadership Skills

- How IT Managers Can Use New Technology To Meet Today's IT Challenges: Technologies That IT Managers Can Use In Order to Make Their Teams More Productive

Negotiating

- The Art Of Packaging A Negotiation: How To Develop The Skill Of Assembling Potential Trades In Order To Get The Best Possible Outcome

- Getting What You Want In A Negotiation By Learning How To Signal: How To Develop The Skill Of Effective Signaling In A Negotiation In Order To Get The Best Possible Outcome

Miscellaneous

- How To Heal A Broken Leg – Fast!: Understanding how to deal with a broken leg in order to start walking again quickly

- How Software Defined Networking (SDN) Is Going To Change Your World Forever: The Revolution In Network Design And How It Affects

Note: See a complete list of books by Dr. Jim Anderson at the back of this book.

Acknowledgements

Any book like this one is the result of years of real-world work experience. In my over 25 years of working for 7 different firms, I have met countless fantastic people and I've been mentored by some truly exceptional ones. Although I've probably forgotten some of the people who made me the person that I am today, here is my attempt to finally give them the recognition that they so truly deserve:

- Thomas P. Anderson
- Art Puett
- Bobbi Marshall
- Bob Boggs

Dr. Jim Anderson

This book is dedicated to my wife Lori. None of this would have been possible without her love and support.

Thanks for the best years of my life (so far)...!

Speaking.   Negotiating.   Managing.   Marketing.

Table Of Contents

What's The Best Way For Politicians To Give A Great Speech?

Being willing to serve takes a real commitment on the part of anyone who wants to be a politician. However, before you can serve, you first have to get elected. In order for that to happen you are going to have to get enough people to believe that your views represent their views. The only way that you'll be able to do this is to prior to the next election, tell them where you stand on the issues that are important to them. There are a lot of different ways to go about doing this, but giving speeches is the time honored way that politicians communicate with the people that they want to vote for them. Now all you have to do is get good at giving speeches and that political office is as good as yours!

Just think of all of the great speakers who have gone before you Dr. Martin Luther King, John F. Kennedy, Steve Jobs, the list goes on and on. Now you've been give your chance to change the world!

I can well image what you are feeling right now – fear, doubt, uncertainty. Don't worry about it. I've got some good news for you – all of those great speakers felt the very same thing. However, they were able to muster up the courage to go out there and give the best speech that they possibly could. They did change the world and you just might end up doing the same thing.

However, before you go doing that, we've got to make sure that you've got a well-planned speech to work with. Planning a speech is the first step in creating and delivering a powerful and effective speech. In order to plan a speech you need to take the time before you start to write out your speech and think about who you'll be speaking to.

When planning a speech you need to make sure that you understand the purpose of your speech. Why are you going to go to all of the effort to create and deliver this speech? After you know that, take the time to think about your audience: what do they want from your speech?

You're going to have to choose what type of speech you want to give. You can choose to deliver an informative speech, a demonstrative speech, an inspirational speech, or a humorous speech. More often than not the speech that you end up giving will draw from all four types of speeches.

The good news is that I know that you're going to give a great speech and it's all going to start with the planning. Take the time to read this book, learn what you need to do in order to plan a great speech and then go out there and knock 'em dead!

Good luck!

-    Dr. Jim Anderson

About The Author

I must confess that I never set out to be a public speaker. When I went to school, I studied Computer Science and thought that I'd get a nice job programming and that would be that. Well, at least part of that plan worked out!

My first job was working for Boeing on their F/A-18 fighter jet program. I spent my days programming fighter jet software in assembly language and I loved it. The U.S. government decided to save some money and went looking for other countries to sell this plane to. This put me into an unfamiliar role: I started to meet with foreign military officials and I ended up having to give speeches in order to explain what my product did.

Time moved on and so did I. I found myself working for Siemens, the big German telecommunications company. They were making phone switches and selling them to the seven U.S. phone companies. The problem was that the switches were too complicated. Customers couldn't tell the difference between one complicated phone switch from another complicated phone switch. Once again I found myself standing in front of the room giving speeches in order to explain what these complicated machines did and why ours were better than anyone else's.

I've spent over 25 years working as a product manager for both big companies and startups. This has given me an opportunity to do many, many presentations for customers, at conferences, and everywhere in-between.

I now live in Tampa Florida where I spend my time managing my consulting business, Blue Elephant Consulting, teaching college courses at the University of South Florida, and traveling to work with companies like yours to share the knowledge that I have about how to create and deliver powerful and effective speeches.

I'm always available to answer questions and I can be reached at:

Dr. Jim Anderson
Blue Elephant Consulting
Email: jim@BlueElephantConsulting.com
Facebook: http://goo.gl/1TVoK
Web: http://www.BlueElephantConsulting.com/

"Unforgettable communication skills that will set your ideas free…"

Create Speeches That Motivate Your Audiences And Get Your Message Heard!

Dr. Jim Anderson is available to provide training and coaching on the topics that are the most important to people who have to speak in public: how can I create a speech that people want to hear and how can I deliver in a way that will allow me to connect with my audience and get my point across to them?

 Dr. Anderson believes that in order to both learn and remember what he says, speakers need to laugh. Each one of his speeches is full of fun and humor so that what he says "sticks" with everyone.

Dr. Anderson's Public Speaking Training Includes:

1. How to plan your next speech: pick your purpose and understand your audience.
2. What's the best way to get PowerPoint and Keynote to work with you, not against you?
3. What do you need to do when you are presenting in order to truly connect with your audience?

Dr. Jim Anderson presents over 100 speeches per year. To invite Dr. Anderson to speak at your event, contact him at:

Phone: 813-418-6970 or
Email: jim@BlueElephantConsulting.com

Chapter 1

Welcome To The Passive Aggressive Games!

We **DO NOT** give a refund on or exchange an item simply because you have changed your mind or "do not like it".

Welcome To The Passive Aggressive Games!

Thanks to millions of years of evolution, we are all pretty good at recognizing situations in which we are called on to compete. Our communication skills are tuned to allow us to make ourselves heard in these situations and to get our point across. Which is why we all seem to do such a poor job when we are faced not with competition, but rather opposition. Oh, oh. What to do now?

So what is opposition? Opposition is what happens when the group of people that you are trying to communicate with are just dead set against what you have to say. If you show up in a situation where you are going to be telling your team about a great new documentation system that the company has mandated that everyone will start using, you will encounter opposition if nobody that you are talking to wants to do documentation in the first place — it's not that the new system is a bad idea (although it might be), it's just that everyone rejects the idea of doing documentation.

What's funny is that although in our field of work we may struggle with how to deal with opposition, the folks who work in politics deal with it on a daily basis. Our elected officials are forced to deal with opposition every day and so they have developed effective ways of dealing with it. We could learn a thing or two from them:

- **Co-opt The Other Side's Issue**: this is one of my favorite approaches. Don't go head-to-head with the opposition. Instead take a careful look at what's motivating their position: why doesn't your team want to do documentation? If you show respect for their underlying issue and then go ahead and propose a different way of solving it, you'll basically cut off the opposition at the knees.

In our documentation case, if you show the team that offshore developers do a poor job of native language documentation and by doing a good job of documentation their work they will be able to keep more jobs onshore, then you've accomplished your co-opting.

- **Redefine The Issue**: Initially an issue may start out as a tug-of-war. In order to solve this problem, if you redefine it in such a way that it is no longer a tug-of-war, then you can win the other side over.

  In our documentation example, the issue could start out as a "the company is telling us to do more work". This could be redefined as "Other companies have created products that interface with our product. In order for them (and us) to be successful, they have to understand how our product works and so documentation is needed." All of a sudden, what was something that was being created for the faceless company becomes a tool for specific small business owners.

If you can become skilled at learning to distinguish opposition from competition, then you will have a hard-to-find skill that you can start to use proactively. Do a little bit of research on the group that you will be communicating with. If there is strong opposition to what you will be discussing with them, it will probably come out quickly. Look for ways to co-opt or redefine the issue and you'll have accomplished half of your job before you even open your mouth.

Chapter 2

"Once Upon A Time..." – The Role Of Storytelling In Business Communication

"Once Upon A Time..." – The Role Of Storytelling In Business Communication

In the eternal quest to communicate better and have our message "stick" with our audience, a powerful tool is often overlooked. A good story, told at the right time, in the right way, to the right audience can have a lasting effect that can transform an organization. Proof of this can be found on the business best seller list over the past few years: "**Who Moved My Cheese**", "**Zapp: The Lightning of Empowerment**", "**A Message From Garcia**", etc. have all proved that everyone loves a good story. Ah, but as always, the devil is in the details. Done wrong, a story can backfire and send your career down in flames. Let's see if we can discover how to tame this wild stallion so that we can ride it to career success.

We've got lots of ways to communicate information, why bother with stories? We all know how to create and use numeric charts and their associated graphs (3-D pie chart anyone?), written reports, etc. A story is the right tool to use when your standard tools just aren't working. Joseph Badaracco, a Harvard Business School professor, says that *"People don't simply hear stories. It triggers things – pictures, thoughts, and associations – in their minds"*. The end result of all of this triggering is that a story can communicate your point in a very powerful way that fully engages your audience.

As always there is a catch. The catch to storytelling is that you need to know where to draw the line between making a dry business story more compelling by embellishing it and changing the story into an outright lie. I can't even begin to stress just how important this rule is. An embellishment is when you transform "I took the test on a hot day" into "As I walked to the most important certification test in my life, the hot Texas sun felt like it was hovering just 10 feet above my head and the melted asphalt splashed as I walked through it." See? You've made a dry story just a bit more interesting. A LIE would be when you say "I worked at ACME products for over 10 years in the Coyote specialty division where I invented the first rocket powered shoes." If you weren't there for 10 years or if you didn't invent that, then that's a lie.

In order for your story to have the impact that you want it to have, it has got to ring true with your audience. If your audience doubts even one part of your story, then they will spend the rest of the time looking for other holes in your tale. However, if your story is true and contains a powerful message that your audience can both picture and feel, then you will have accomplished what very few other communicators can do — you will have gotten your message across.

Chapter 3

Arrgh! Isn't There A Law Against Giving Bad Presentations?

Arrgh! Isn't There A Law Against Giving Bad Presentations?

I probably need to apologize in advance for this rant — I've finally reached my breaking point.

I somehow got myself trapped in a presentation on changes to my 401k retirement program. I guess that I should start by admitting that I really can't think of a much more boring topic to talk about in the first place even though I know that I should be really interested because, after all, it is my retirement.

However, the person giving the presentation was beyond bad — they were just awful. To make matters worse, the presentation went on for over 1-1/2 hours. Well before the end I was wondering if I could sneak out the back door, but alas, it was not to be.

When I finally stumbled out of this colossal waste of time, I found myself wondering how I could avoid getting trapped in any such presentations in the future. Yes, I did for just a minute dream of a world in which presentation police would show up and arrest anyone who did a poor or careless job of presenting information. I was thinking that the charge would have to be something along the lines of "… *intent to do bodily harm.*"

Since we don't live in that world, what do ALL presenters of complex information need to know (we'll leave motivational speakers out of it for now)? At the end of the day I believe that there are two critical skills that all speakers must have: (1) the ability to understand and use how adults learn when constructing a speech, and (2) the ability to appeal to all types of learning methods during the same presentation.

The days of sitting in school and having a teacher talk at us are over. We get bombarded with way too much information every day. Ultimately, I believe that it's the presenter's responsibility to deliver information in a way that we can understand and remember it. So there you go, there are no presentation police, but if there were would you have an arrest record?

Chapter 4

The Art And Science Of Persuasion

The Art And Science Of Persuasion

So why do we even bother communicating information to others? The answer is simple: we often need others to see things the way that we do. Study after study has shown that most people (myself included) believe that we're so smart that we cannot be sold. The great communicators know that the truth turns out to be that we can be persuaded to do something if, and only if, we don't recognize that a "sales" technique is being used on us.

Why should this matter to you? Simple – when you are presenting information and you take the time to incorporate a few persuasion techniques then you are taking advantage of what modern psychological research has revealed about how we can make the message that we're delivering both more credible and believable. Let's talk about how you can accomplish this...

- **Use a rifle, not a shotgun:** If you want your audience to accept your ideas and make them their own, you need to aim at a narrow target. This means that you need to stop doing what we all instinctively do: back the truck up and dump everything that we know about a topic all over our audience. It turns out that this will just end up overwhelming them and not do much to bring them over to our side.

  Instead, what you should do is some field work before you present your information and find out what's important to your audience. This will allow you to focus your persuasion on those and only those points.

- **<u>Make It Story Time</u>**: Stories are a fantastic way for us to learn and they can be very effective way to persuade someone. However, if it sounds like you are giving a sales pitch, then you can be assured that telling a story won't work.

  Instead, if you focus on a story that has real meaning, then your audience's unconscious mind will automatically draw the necessary connections without any help from you and the result will be that they end up doing the persuasion for you. The key to telling an effective story is to once again pinpoint what matters to your audience and then tell a story about a similar idea or concept. This indirect approach is the secret to winning your audience over to your side and keeps them from feeling like you are selling to them.

Chapter 5

Going Global: How To Give A Presentation Internationally

Going Global: How To Give A Presentation Internationally

As if being a public speaker for a day wasn't hard enough, just try taking yourself out of your home territory and plopping you down somewhere else in the world. Can you just image the amount of trouble that you could get yourself into quickly?

We work hard to create a presentation that will capture the imagination of our audience and cause them to take some sort of action. However, as we are building our speech, we have a habit of imagining our audience as being like us. If we travel to somewhere else in the world and deliver a presentation, then all of a sudden this very basic assumption is no longer correct and we may find ourselves in hot water. Let's see if there are some tips on how to handle international presentations...

Terri Morrison is an author who has written a couple of books on the topic of delivering international presentations and so she really knows her stuff. As with all speaking opportunities, the secret to your success is to study ahead of time. Here are three tips from Terri that will help make your international presentation a success:

1. **Careful With Names**: We probably don't spend that much time thinking about names in our everyday life. We get introduced to people and then we just start calling them by their first names: "Bob", "Ann", etc. Well it turns out that is exactly the wrong way to handle names when you are presenting internationally.

    In the rest of the world, names are treated with a

great deal of respect. Often times a person's name has a lot of family history worked into it. Morrison points out that in many European cultures a person's parent's names are worked into their names – this means that you can easily insult more than just one person if you screw-up pronouncing their name.

Assumptions will also trip you up. In China, the family name comes before the middle name which then comes before the last name. This means that the leader of China, Hu Jintao, would be addressed as Mr. Hu, NOT Mr. Jintao!

In one of my favorite countries, Germany, people are very, very formal with their names. Basically, outside of the home you would never use someone's first name to address them – you always refer to them as "Mr. Smith", not "John". Oh, and one more thing – get the pronunciation of the name correct. This just might be the most important thing that you do!

2. **Would You Like A Date?:** This is a small point that can have a huge impact. In the U.S. we like to write the date in month, day, and year format: 11/02/08. In Europe, the date is written in day, month, year format: 02/11/08.

Just to make things really confusing, Morrison reports that in China and Hong Kong dates are written in year, month, day format: 08/11/02. How to prevent this from becoming a problem during your presentation? I suggest that you always write out dates: November, 2nd, 2008. This way there can be no confusion.

3. **<u>Watch That Dancing</u>**: This may be the most difficult point of all. Non-verbal communication is a critical part of all of our presentations. However, just like spoken language, non-verbal communication differs in every part of the world.

   Lots of us like to use BIG gestures during our presentations so that the folks at the back of the room can see what we are doing. However, this can be the wrong move in countries like Japan. In Japan, subtlety is how communication is done and so it's your little movements that the audience will be looking for, not the big over the top ones. Your best bet is to basically try to move as little as possible during your presentation so as to not inadvertently send the wrong signal to your audience.

Being asked to take your presentation on the road should be seen as a great compliment. However, you need to be aware that you are not in Kansas anymore Dorothy. Your best bet for avoiding offending your audience and allowing your words to do your talking for you is to get a local mentor. This would be someone who understands where you are coming from and who understands your local audience. They can share with you the do's and don'ts of how best to deliver an effective presentation ... and isn't that really why you are there?

Chapter 6

How To Make A Technical
Presentation Riveting

How To Make A Technical Presentation Riveting

So who among us ever really looks forward to sitting through a technical presentation? Collectively we've all sat through so many of these things that we almost defensively shut down before the speaker even has a chance to get started.

So when it's our turn to talk about things that contain lots of financial details, construction details, manufacturing details, procedure details, etc. it's quite common for our blood to run cold because we realize that now the shoe is on the other foot – we are going to be the ones who are boring the audience!

Why are these types of presentations so hard to do? In all honesty, the problem really lies with the presenter, not the audience. Specifically what they all seem to be doing wrong is that they've made the mistake of thinking that they are just having a talk with coworkers: they show up to share information. Big mistake.

Nobody ever shows up for a presentation hoping to have the presenter share information with them. Instead, they are showing up so that the presenter can tell them what they need to do. They may not agree with what they are being told to do, but that is what they are looking for.

What this means for the presenter is that he/she needs to understand that the goal of the presentation is for action to be taken by the audience based on the information that was in the presentation. It really is that simple!

Professional speaker Anne Warfield has come up with three ways to make your next technical presentation even more riveting (and I've added a suggestion of my own). Let's take a look and see what you need to do in order to keep your audience on the edge of their seats next time you talk technical:

- **What's The Next Step?**: When you are creating your technical presentation, you need to start at the end. Once you are done with your presentation, what action do you want your audience to take or what conclusion do you want them to have reached? If you don't have a clear understanding of this, then you'll end up filling your presentation with a discussion about HOW you reached your results and that is what everyone will end up talking about.

- **What Question Do You Need To Answer?**: If you've been able figure out what action you want your audience to take once you are done, then the next step is to understand what questions or objections might be preventing them from taking that next step either right now or after you are done. This is the question (or questions) that your presentation needs to provide answers to.

- **Make It Real**: The technical topic that you are talking about may or may not be familiar to all of your audience. If you can "map" it to something that they are all familiar with, then all of a sudden the audience's comprehension of what you are talking about will go up dramatically.

- **Match Your Audience**: The amount of technical detail in your speech and your use of technical terms and acronyms needs to be matched to your audience. If you assume too little, then they will quickly become bored by your too basic discussion. If you assume too much, then they will become lost in a sea of terms that they don't recognize. Get it right and you'll be connected to your audience from the get go.

Your next technical presentation does not have to be dry and boring. Use these tips BEFORE you give the presentation in order to ensure that your presentation will be riveting and talked about long after you are done.

Chapter 7

Hey Good Looking – Are You A Presenter?

Hey Good Looking – Are You A Presenter?

When we deliver a presentation, we need to make the best use of all of the tools that we have at our disposal. These tools include things such as hand gestures, using pauses, and vocal variety. All too often we forget that we have one more tool for us to use: our personal style.

Life is busy and all too often too many of us just don't take the time to look our best when we venture out into public. The reasons for this are many – we don't expect to meet anyone that we know, we don't think that we're going to be out for long, or maybe we just don't care.

It turns out that this kind of thinking opens all sorts of doors for us as presenters. If we take the time to look our best then we'll end up being the best looking person in the room. What this means is that everyone will be looking at us. If they are already looking at us, then we've got half of our presenting task taken care of!

Carmine Gallo is a communications coach who has spent a lot of time thinking about this topic. Here are some of his suggestions that will help you use this tool to its fullest extent:

- **Keep The Bling To A Minimum**: Over time we all build up a collection of accessories. Women have a collection of flashy necklaces and too-big earrings. Men have (also) too flashy necklaces, tie holders, bracelets, etc. Remember that accessories are designed to add value to your look – not to distract from the overall package. The rule is to keep it simple and suitable for your outfit.

- **Get Some Culture**: This should be something that your research for any presentation reveals to you. A suit is always appropriate – except when it's not. Make sure that you dress in a way that matches the event or the culture of your audience. Have your dress match the expectations of your audience.

- **Smile For The Camera**: As long as you are going to the effort of getting all gussied up for your big presentation, take the time to make sure that all of the photographs that are taken of you show how good you look. We can never have enough photos of ourselves when we are looking our bests. Find a professional photographer and get a formal picture taken of yourself – this will be invaluable to you later on.

All too often we end up spending all of our time researching what we want to say, how we want to say it, and what we want our audience to be motivated to do once we are done talking.

If we take the time to plan out how we are going to look for our next presentation then we'll be ahead of the game before we even show up. Sometimes just taking the time to look at ourselves in the mirror before we head out the door can do wonders for making our presentation that much more effective...!

Chapter 8

Do You Look Presentable During Your Presentation?

Do You Look Presentable During Your Presentation?

Remember when your Mom said that looks don't matter? She may have been right then; however, now is now and the better you look, the more impact your presentation will have.

Whether you realize it or not, you are always being judged by your audience. What you need is some advice to make sure that you come out on top when they judge you. If you take a moment and think about it, you are representing a brand in how you act, walk, and talk. Your wardrobe plays a big part in the impression that you make.

Carmine Gallo is a communications coach who has spent a lot of time thinking about this topic. Here are some of his suggestions that will help you do this correctly:

- **You MUST Look Better Than Everyone Else In The Room:** If you remember nothing else from this article, then remember this – great presenters should always dress just a little bit nicer than everyone else who is attending the event. The classic example of this was the U.S. president Ronald Reagan ("the great communicator") who always stood out because he was always the best dressed person in the room.

- **Make Sure That Your Clothes Fit Correctly**: How many of us wear clothes that are too short, too long, too tight, or even too loose? If you'll take just a moment and list to what George Zimmerman, the founder of Men's Wearhouse, says you'll understand that you are making a mistake. Zimmerman says that the #1 most important decision that you need to make when buying clothes is that they give you a proper fit.

- **<u>Make Sure Your Clothes Say Nice Things About You</u>**: Make sure that you choose clothes that complement you – your skin tone, hair, and your eye color. The key here is to make sure that your clothes complement you, not fight you. Feel free to mix and match – just make sure that they look good together.

- **<u>Are You Well Heeled?</u>:** Assuming that you are not a puppy, it is still important that you pay attention to your shoes. It turns out that people really do notice the shoes that you are wearing. Make sure that you spend as much time on picking out your shoes as you do the rest of your outfit.

- **<u>Quality Is Worth It – Spend More</u>**: It turns out that you are not just paying for a fancy designer label. High quality fabrics and shoes not only look better, but they also last longer. Go ahead – spend more for better quality clothes and you'll not only look nicer, but you will save money in the end because your clothes will last longer.

There you go – it's not that hard to look great. Take the time to look good and your presentation will have that much more impact.

Chapter 9

How To Present On The Worst Day Of Your Life

How To Present On The Worst Day Of Your Life

The real secret to giving a good presentation is for the presenter to be "up" and have a great deal of energy. Under the best of circumstances, this can be a challenge to do, if you've had a really bad day it can appear to be darn near impossible.

So what's a presenter to do? Fran Capo is a motivational speaker / comedian who has had to face these types of situations. Ultimately it's all mental – you've got to get yourself into the right frame of mind. Sounds easy doesn't it? In reality if you don't know how to do this, it can be quite hard.

Fran has a number of suggestions for how we can gather our wits about ourselves on the worst days of our lives and still deliver a knockout presentation:

- **Breathe Correctly**: when things start to go bad for us we screw up our breathing – we take too many short breaths. Realize this and stop, take a moment to focus on your breath, and take a few deep, long breaths. This will start to calm you down.

- **Adjust Your Attitude**: How you choose to view a situation is entirely up to you. No matter how bad the day has been so far, you are in control of how the rest of it turns out. Realizing this and forcing yourself to think positively is the key to making your presentation come off perfectly.

- **Put It In A Box**: I can't tell you how many times I've gotten bad news just before I was to go on and give a presentation. In order to prevent life's little hand grenades from destroying your presentation, you need to learn to put your negative emotions in a box and slam it shut when you don't have time to worry about them. However, be sure to open it later on and process your emotions when you have the time.

We can't prevent life from handing us lemons before, during, or after our presentations. However, with a little care and some understanding of how we deal with bad news, the show can still go on.

Chapter 10

Persuade An Audience Using 3 Secrets Used By Presenters

Persuade An Audience Using 3 Secrets Used By Presenters

If you think about it, there are a lot of different types of speeches that we can give: humorous, informative, motivational, and of course, ones that are designed to get your audience to start thinking a particular way. Oh yeah, this last type just may be the hardest type of speech to give...

Where Do You Start When You Want To Persuade?

At its very heart, persuasion is the art of getting your audience to see the world the same way that you do. As all of us speakers know, no matter if you are talking to a graduation or a business gathering, an audience is not a single entity – it's a lot of different people sitting out there who all have different opinions on any given topic. Your job as a speaker is to win over as many of them to your side as possible.

Pick Your Problem

John Coleman is an author and a former U.S. national speech champion who knows a thing or two about how to build a speech that can persuade. Coleman points out that before you can have any hope of persuading an audience, both of you need to agree that there is a problem in the first place.

As obvious as this may seem, you could talk until you are blue in the face and it would all be for naught if your audience didn't agree with you that there is a problem. In order to get your audience to agree that there is a problem that needs to be solved, you need to do three things:

1. Isolate it & limit its scope
2. Make it urgent
3. Make it significant

You Got To Keep 'Em Isolated

Have you ever heard that phrase "You can't boil the ocean"? When it comes to persuading an audience it applies – you need to make sure that you pick a problem that you can actually do something about. Scope down a bigger problem ("world hunger") to something that your audience can do something about ("hunger in our town").

Run!

Well, don't run but you do want to convince your audience that they need to take action. Just talking about a problem isn't enough to cause your audience to actually agree to DO anything. Somehow you are going to have to lite a fire underneath them so that they will end up taking some action (that's why it's called "persuasion"!)

It's Only A Problem If It's Significant

Assuming that you've been able to convince your audience that there is a problem, your next step is to make sure that you bring it home – you've got to relate the problem to their lives. This is going to require that you have an understanding of who your audience is so that you can describe to them how this problem is going to affect them in terms that will motivate them to take action.

Final Thoughts

Speeches that persuade are not easy speeches to give. However, as with so many things in life – it's the ability to do the hard things that make us more valuable. If you take the time to understand how to prepare to give an effective persuasive speech, then you'll have a powerful new speaking tool and you'll be able to intimately connect with your audience and make a lasting impact in their lives.

Chapter 11

Persuasion Power – How To Win Over An Audience

Persuasion Power – How To Win Over An Audience

Not all speeches are the same. Graduations, weddings, corporate pep-rally's – those are all pretty straightforward. One of the most difficult types of speeches to give is one in which you have been brought in to convince an audience of something. As difficult as this type of speech is to give, if you can become good at doing it, you will seen as being a very valuable speaker indeed!

Persuasion Starts With Small Steps

You can assume that the audience that you'll be speaking to will be made up of a mix of people who already support your position, who have not make up their minds yet, and who are dead set against whatever you are going to say. Good luck with that!

Clearly the first step in winning any audience over is for you to do your homework BEFORE you are facing the audience. One key area to research is to find out what arguments "the other side" has made. If there is a person or a group that represents "the other side", then this is pretty straightforward. If there is not a clear "other side", then you're going to have to spend some time researching the flip side of what you want to persuade your audience about – because some people will have decided that that is what they want to believe.

One sure-fire way to start to win your audience over to your way of thinking is by using something called strategic agreement. When you do this you agree with parts of the other side's position. Automatically this will start to make the audience view you as a reasonable person. They may not completely agree with you, but they will start to warm to your view point.

Show Up Ready For A Fight

Well, maybe that's putting it just a little bit too harshly. How about if we say that you need to show up ready to address your audience's objections. Whatever you have been asked to convince them about, there will be objections to it. Before you give your speech, you need to once again do your homework. In your speech you need to make sure that you address each of these objections.

Sometimes we like to shy away from sticky arguments that we don't feel that we have a good response to. However, you must be careful to not do this. It turns out that if you don't address an objection, then your audience will assume that it is a valid objection because you didn't talk about it.

This Is A No Dumping Zone

I am probably more guilty of dumping than anyone else that I know. When I'm giving a persuasive speech, I want to make sure that I get my point across. This means that I'll do a lot of research and, if I'm not careful, I'll "dump" all of that research on my audience during my presentation. This is a bad idea.

Instead, you want to do the research, pick out the points that are going to be the most important to your audience, and then use your research to support you when your cover just these few points in detail.

What It Takes To Make A Good Argument

You would think that we'd all know this by now, but when I'm coaching speakers I keep discovering that they know WHAT they want to say to make their point, but they don't know HOW to say it. It turns out that there is a simple formula that allows you to create a complete argument in order to support your position:

- **First: Make An Assertion** – you've got to tell your audience what point you are going to be trying to convince them about. Without this, they'll never know what you are talking about.

- **Next: Tell Them Why** – this is where you need to explain to your audience why YOU think that your position is correct. This is the meat of your point and you really need to come across as convincing.

- **Finally: Show Proof** - the fact that you believe something is great, but not enough. You need to wrap up your point by sharing evidence with your audience that will back up your position.

Final Thoughts

There is no doubt about it – winning people over to your way of thinking is just about the hardest type of speech to give. Ask any politician. However, it can be done. What it requires is that you do a lot of homework in order to prepare your arguments with an understanding of the facts and what your audience is currently thinking.

Public speaking is never an easy thing to do. Developing the skills that are needed in order to rally a crowd behind a new idea, a change in policy, or bold new idea is time well spent for a speaker. If you can do this, then you'll have a powerful new speaking tool and you'll be able to intimately connect with your audience and make a lasting impact in their lives.

Chapter 12

Know Your Audience: What You Don't Know May Hurt You

Know Your Audience:
What You Don't Know May Hurt You

When you think of the perfect speech in your mind, what do you see? Do you see yourself up on a stage giving a speech, reaching the end, and then having everyone stand up and applaud until their hands grow tired? Nice picture. However, all too often that doesn't happen. There are lots of reasons for this, but one big one is because we don't take the time to fully know our audience...

Why Bother?

Why give a speech in the first place? There always has to be a reason for us to give a speech – are we there to entertain, inform, motivate, etc. We won't be able to do this if we don't connect with our audience. We won't be able to connect with our audience if we don't know who they are.

It's way too easy for a speaker to make assumptions about the audiences that we are talking to. The biggest mistake is to assume that they see the world the way that we do. Craig Harrison points out that by presuming that the audience thinks the way that we do we risk offending them – perhaps without even realizing it.

It Takes A Village To Give A Speech

The right way to go about getting an audience on your side is to tackle three big issues right off the bat in any speech that you are giving:

1. **Acknowledge Differences**: What makes you different from the majority of your audience? You realize this and your audience realizes it. Deal with it in a way that shows respect. If you are an older speaker talking to a much younger audience you could start out by saying "I realize that you are out there looking at me and thinking to yourself that I may be old enough to be your parent; however, don't worry – I won't be telling you that you should visit your mother more often, that you really should be getting more sleep, or asking when you'll finally be getting married. Instead, how about if we talk about…"

2. **Include Everyone**: Not only are you an outsider to your audience, there is a good chance that a lot of people in your audience are outsiders to the rest of the audience. Use the opening of your speech to unite everyone together at least on a single issue. An example might be "I realize that we all live in different neighborhoods, go to different schools, and attend different churches, but the proposed change in how property taxes are calculated will affect us all and that's what I'd like to talk to you about tonight."

3. **Mind Your Reputation**: Before you even open your mouth, the audience has pre-judged you. It might be based on the information that was used to advertise the event or perhaps you are known for some past deed. Dealing with this right off the bat will allow your audience to get by it and start to listen to what you have to say. One way to do this would be "I come from the sunny state of Florida where you might think

that just about everyone is retired and just living off of Medicare. However, there are a few of us who are still working and we care just as much, if not more, about the current debate over healthcare reform…"

Final Thoughts

Giving a speech is a tough job. Giving a good speech is even tougher. You need to have your audience working with you, not against you if you want to have any hope of making an impact. The first step in accomplishing this is realizing that your audience is different from you.

Once you acknowledge this, then you need to work to include them and dispel any preconceived ideas that they may have about you. Learn to do this well and you'll be able to intimately connect with your audience and make a lasting impact in their lives.

Hard work does not
guarantee success;
However, success does
not happen
without hard work.

- Dr. Jim Anderson

Create Speeches That Motivate Your Audiences And Get Your Message Heard!

Dr. Jim Anderson is available to provide training and coaching on the topics that are the most important to people who have to speak in public: how can I create a speech that people want to hear and how can I deliver in a way that will allow me to connect with my audience and get my point across to them?

Dr. Anderson believes that in order to both learn and remember what he says, speakers need to laugh. Each one of his speeches is full of fun and humor so that what he says "sticks" with everyone.

Dr. Anderson's Public Speaking Training Includes:

1. How to plan your next speech: pick your purpose and understand your audience.
2. What's the best way to get PowerPoint and Keynote to work with you, not against you?
3. What do you need to do when you are presenting in order to truly connect with your audience?

Dr. Jim Anderson presents over 100 speeches per year. To invite Dr. Anderson to speak at your event, contact him at:

Phone: 813-418-6970 or
Email: jim@BlueElephantConsulting.com

Blue Elephant Consulting
Speaking. Negotiating. Managing. Market

Photo Credits:

Cover - By: Samurai Juan Follow

https://www.flickr.com/photos/samuraijuan/

Chapter 1 - By: James Whatley

http://www.flickr.com/photos/whatleydude/

Chapter 2 - By: digistorytellin

http://www.flickr.com/photos/digistorytellin/

Chapter 3 - By: Alan Levine

http://www.flickr.com/photos/cogdog/

Chapter 4 - By: Neal

http://www.flickr.com/photos/nealoneal/

Chapter 5 - By: Steve Cadman

http://www.flickr.com/photos/stevecadman/

Chapter 6 - By: Junya Ogura

http://www.flickr.com/photos/sooey/

Chapter 7 - By: Balanda

http://www.flickr.com/photos/balanda/

Chapter 8 - By: Susan Sermoneta

http://www.flickr.com/photos/en321/

Chapter 9 - By: Adam Fagen

http://www.flickr.com/photos/afagen/

Chapter 10 - By: kulucphr

http://www.flickr.com/photos/kulucphr/

Chapter 11 - By: UK Parliament

http://www.flickr.com/photos/uk_parliament/

Chapter 12 - By: Shane Kelly

http://www.flickr.com/photos/29106784@N02/

Other Books By The Author

Product Management

- Manage Your Customers, Manage Your Product: Techniques For Product Managers To Better Understand What Their Customers Really Want

- How Product Managers Can Sell More Of Their Product: Tips & Techniques For Product Managers To Better Understand How To Sell Their Product

- How Product Managers Can Sell More Of Their Product: Tips & Techniques For Product Managers To Better Understand How To Sell Their Product

- How To Create A Successful Product That Customers Will Want: Techniques For Product Managers To Boost Product Sales And Increase Customer Satisfaction

- What Product Managers Need To Know About World-Class Product Development: How Product Managers Can Create Successful Products

- How Product Managers Can Learn To Understand Their Customers: Techniques For Product

Managers To Better Understand What Their
Customers Really Want

- Product Management Secrets: Techniques For
  Product Managers To Boost Product Sales And
  Increase Customer Satisfaction

- Product Development Lessons For Product
  Managers: How Product Managers Can Create
  Successful Products

- Customer Lessons For Product Managers:
  Techniques For Product Managers To Better
  Understand What Their Customers Really Want

- Product Failure Lessons For Product Managers:
  Examples Of Products That Have Failed For Product
  Managers To Learn From

- Communication Skills For Product Managers: The
  Communication Skills That Product Managers Need
  To Know How To Use In Order To Have A Successful
  Product

- How To Have A Successful Product Manager
  Career: The Things That You Need To Be Doing
  TODAY In Order To Have A Successful Product
  Manager Career

- Product Manager Product Success: How to keep your product on track and make it become a success

Public Speaking

- How To Get Ready To Give The Perfect Speech: What Tools To Use To Create Your Next Speech So That Your Message Will Be Remembered Forever!

- Creating Speeches That Work: How To Create A Speech That Will Make Your Message Be Remembered Forever!

- How To Organize A Speech In Order To Make Your Point: How to put together a speech that will capture and hold your audience's attention

- Changing How You Speak To Overcome Your Fear Of Speaking: Change techniques that will transform a speech into a memorable event

- Delivering Excellence: How To Give Presentations That Make A Difference: Presentation techniques that will transform a speech into a memorable event

- Tools Speakers Need In Order To Give The Perfect Speech: What tools to use to create your next speech so that your message will be remembered forever!

- How To Create A Speech That Will Be Remembered

- Secrets To Organizing A Speech For Maximum Impact: How to put together a speech that will capture and hold your audience's attention

- How To Become A Better Speaker By Changing How You Speak: Change techniques that will transform a speech into a memorable event

- How To Give A Great Presentation: Presentation techniques that will transform a speech into a memorable event

- How To Rehearse In Order To Give The Perfect Speech: How to effectively rehearse your next speech to that your message be remembered forever!

- Secrets To Creating The Perfect Speech: How to create a speech that will make your message be remembered forever!

- Secrets To Organizing The Perfect Speech: How to organize the best speech of your life!

- Secrets To Planning The Perfect Speech: How to plan to give the best speech of your life

- How To Show What You Mean During A Presentation: How to use visual techniques to transform a speech into a memorable event

CIO Skills

- How CIOs Can Take Their Career To The Next Level: How CIOs Can Work With The Entire Company In Order To Be Successful

- How CIOs Can Bring Business And IT Together: How CIOs Can Use Their Technical Skills To Help Their Company Solve Real-World Business Problems

- New IT Technology Issues Facing CIOs: How CIOs Can Stay On Top Of The Changes In The Technology That Powers The Company

- Keeping The Barbarians Out: How CIOs Can Secure Their Department and Company: Tips And Techniques For CIOs To Use In Order To Secure Both Their IT Department And Their Company

- What CIOs Need To Know In Order To Successfully Manage An IT Department: Decision Making Skills That Every CIO Needs To Have In Order To Be Able

To Make The Right Choices

- Becoming A Powerful And Effective Leader: Tips And Techniques That IT Managers Can Use In Order To Develop Leadership Skills

- CIO Secrets For Growing Innovation: Tips And Techniques For CIOs To Use In Order To Make Innovation Happen In Their IT Department

- Your Success As A CIO Depends On How Well You Communicate: Tips And Techniques For CIOs To Use In Order To Become Better Communicators

- What CIOs Need To Know About Working With Partners: Techniques For CIOs To Use In Order To Be Able To Successfully Work With Partners

- Critical CIO Management Skills: Decision Making Skills That Every CIO Needs To Have In Order To Be Able To Make The Right Choices

- How CIOs Can Make Innovation Happen: Tips And Techniques For CIOs To Use In Order To Make Innovation Happen In Their IT Department

- CIO Communication Skills Secrets: Tips And Techniques For CIOs To Use In Order To Become

Better Communicators

- Managing Your CIO Career: Steps That CIOs Have To Take In Order To Have A Long And Successful Career

- CIO Business Skills: How CIOs can work effectively with the rest of the company!

IT Manager Skills

- Understanding What Leadership Means For IT Managers: Tips And Techniques That IT Managers Can Use In Order To Develop Leadership Skills

- How IT Managers Can Use New Technology To Meet Today's IT Challenges: Technologies That IT Managers Can Use In Order to Make Their Teams More Productive

- How To Build High Performance IT Teams: Tips And Techniques That IT Managers Can Use In Order To Develop Productive Teams

- Save Yourself, Save Your Job – How To Manage Your IT Career: Secrets That IT Managers Can Use In Order To Have A Successful Career

- Growing Your CIO Career: How CIOs Can Work With The Entire Company In Order To Be Successful

- How IT Managers Can Make Innovation Happen: Tips And Techniques For IT Managers To Use In Order To Make Innovation Happen In Their Teams

- Staffing Skills IT Managers Must Have: Tips And Techniques That IT Managers Can Use In Order To Correctly Staff Their Teams

- Secrets Of Effective Leadership For IT Managers: Tips And Techniques That IT Managers Can Use In Order To Develop Leadership Skills

- IT Manager Career Secrets: Tips And Techniques That IT Managers Can Use In Order To Have A Successful Career

- IT Manager Budgeting Skills: How IT Managers Can Request, Manage, Use, And Track Their Funding

- Secrets Of Managing Budgets: What IT Managers Need To Know In Order To Understand How Their Company Uses Money

Negotiating

- The Art Of Packaging A Negotiation: How To Develop The Skill Of Assembling Potential Trades In Order To Get The Best Possible Outcome

- Getting What You Want In A Negotiation By Learning How To Signal: How To Develop The Skill Of Effective Signaling In A Negotiation In Order To Get The Best Possible Outcome

- Exploring How To Get The Deal That You Want In A Negotiation: How To Develop The Skill Of Exploring What Is Possible In A Negotiation In Order To Reach The Best Possible Deal

- Use The Power Of Arguing To Win Your Next Negotiation: How To Develop The Skill Of Effective Arguing In A Negotiation In Order To Get The Best Possible Outcome

- Learn How To Signal In Your Next Negotiation: How To Develop The Skill Of Effective Signaling In A Negotiation In Order To Get The Best Possible Outcome

- Learn The Skill Of Exploring In A Negotiation: How To Develop The Skill Of Exploring What Is Possible In A Negotiation In Order To Reach The Best

Possible Deal

- Learn How To Argue In Your Next Negotiation: How To Develop The Skill Of Effective Arguing In A Negotiation In Order To Get The Best Possible Outcome|

- How To Open Your Next Negotiation: How To Start A Negotiation In Order To Get The Best Possible Outcome

- Preparing For Your Next Negotiation: What You Need To Do BEFORE A Negotiation Starts In Order To Get The Best Possible Deal

- Learn How To Package Trades In Your Next Negotiation

- All Good Things Come To An End: How To Close A Negotiation - How To Develop The Skill Of Closing In Order To Get The Best Possible Outcome From A Negotiation

- Take No Prisoners In Your Next Negotiation: How To Start A Negotiation In Order To Get The Best Possible Outcome

Miscellaneous

- How To Heal A Broken Leg – Fast!: Understanding how to deal with a broken leg in order to start walking again quickly

- How Software Defined Networking (SDN) Is Going To Change Your World Forever: The Revolution In Network Design And How It Affects You

- The Power Of Virtualization: How It Affects Memory, Servers, and Storage: The Revolution In Creating Virtual Devices And How It Affects You

- The Internet-Enabled Successful School District Superintendent: How To Use The Internet To Boost Parental Involvement In Your Schools

- Power Distribution Unit (PDU) Secrets: What Everyone Who Works In A Data Center Needs To Know!

- Making The Jump: How To Land Your Dream Job When You Get Out Of College!

- How To Use The Internet To Create Successful Students And Involved Parents

"How to plan to give the best speech of your life!"

This book has been written with one goal in mind – to show you how you can make your next speech a success. It's not easy being a public speaker so we're going to show you what you need to be doing in order to make your next speech stand out, generate interest, and get you heard!

Let's Make Your Next Speech A Success!

What You'll Find Inside:

- **"ONCE UPON A TIME…" – THE ROLE OF STORYTELLING IN BUSINESS COMMUNICATION**

- **HOW TO MAKE A TECHNICAL PRESENTATION RIVETING**

- **PERSUADE AN AUDIENCE USING 3 SECRETS USED BY PRESENTERS**

- **KNOW YOUR AUDIENCE: WHAT YOU DON'T KNOW MAY HURT YOU**

Dr. Jim Anderson brings his 25 years of real-world experience to this book. He's delivered speeches at some of the world's largest firms as well as at many conferences. He's going to show you what you need to do in order to make your next speech a success!